It's My State!

MINNESOTA
The Land of 10,000 Lakes

Marlene Brill and Elizabeth Kaplan

Cavendish
Square
New York

Published in 2015 by Cavendish Square Publishing, LLC
243 5th Avenue, Suite 136, New York, NY 10016

Copyright © 2015 by Cavendish Square Publishing, LLC

Third Edition

Website: cavendishsq.com

This publication represents the opinions and views of the author based on his or her personal experience, knowledge, and research. The information in this book serves as a general guide only. The author and publisher have used their best efforts in preparing this book and disclaim liability rising directly or indirectly from the use and application of this book.

CPSIA Compliance Information: Batch #WS14CSQ

All websites were available and accurate when this book was sent to press.

Library of Congress Cataloging-in-Publication Data
Brill, Marlene Targ.
 Minnesota / Marlene Brill, Elizabeth Kaplan. — [Third edition].
    pages cm. — (It's my state!)
 Includes index.
 ISBN 978-1-62712-748-6 (hardcover) ISBN 978-1-62712-751-6 (ebook)
 1. Minnesota—Juvenile literature. I. Kaplan, Elizabeth, 1956- II. Title.

F606.3.B75 2014
977.6—dc23

2014012956

Editorial Director: Dean Miller
Editor, Third Edition: Nicole Sothard
Art Director: Jeffrey Talbot
Series Designer, Third Edition: Jeffrey Talbot
Layout Design, Third Edition: Erica Clendening
Production Manager: Jennifer Ryder-Talbot

Printed in the United States of America

MINNESOTA

CONTENTS

State Tree: Norway Pine

Most of the Norway pines in Minnesota are found in the northern and northeastern parts of the state. As the tree ages, the bark begins to turn reddish, which is why this tree is also known as the red pine. Minnesota's tallest red pine is 120 feet (37 meters) tall and over 300 years old.

State Bird: Common Loon

This black-and-white bird can be seen gliding gently across Minnesota lakes. One of the world's oldest surviving bird species, loons can dive more than 100 feet (30 m) underwater in search of food and can stay underwater for nearly five minutes. Minnesota has more loons than any other state except Alaska.

State Flower: Pink and White Lady's Slipper

Lady's slippers dot Minnesota's wetlands, bogs, and forests with their beautiful pink-and-white bowl-like flowers. The plants grow slowly, taking four to sixteen years to flower. They may live for up to 100 years and grow 4 feet (1.2 m) tall. It is illegal to pick this flower without permission.

State Muffin: Blueberry

In 1988, a group of third-grade children in the town of Carlton convinced the state **legislature** to make the blueberry muffin the State Muffin. Wild blueberries grow in the swamps, forests, and hills of northeastern Minnesota.

State Gemstone: Lake Superior Agate

Lake Superior agate is found in rocks that formed billions of years ago. This mineral is known for the beautiful lines of red, yellow, and orange that form designs in it. The lines are thin bands of iron. Pieces of agate are often polished and used in jewelry.

State Drink: Milk

Minnesota cows produce around 9 billion pounds (4 billion kilograms) of milk each year. The state generally ranks fifth or sixth in the nation for milk production. So it makes sense that Minnesotans chose milk as their state drink.

Boaters canoe on one of Minnesota's
many beautiful lakes.

The Land of 10,000 Lakes

Minnesota has sky-blue waters, blankets of forest, and acres of sweeping **fertile** flatland. The state's different terrains, plus a wide range of weather from north to south, make Minnesota seem like several states in one. It is the fourteenth largest state, with a land area of 79,610 square miles (206,189 square kilometers).

The name "Minnesota" comes from a Dakota word meaning "water that reflects the sky." Known as the "Land of 10,000 Lakes," Minnesota really has more than 20,000 lakes.

Where did all the lakes and rivers come from? Scientists say that about 11,000 to 12,000 years ago, most of Minnesota was covered by glaciers—huge sheets of slow-moving ice. As the glaciers moved in, they flattened hills and dug out valleys. As they moved out, they deposited soil, sand, and rocks and left behind many holes filled with ice. Lakes formed when the ice melted. Rivers formed as the melting ice drained away.

Minnesota can be divided into four geographic regions, based on the main **ecosystem** in each region. Mixed forests of evergreen and deciduous trees (those that lose their leaves in the fall) cover northeastern and north-central Minnesota. Deciduous forests extend in a diagonal band from the northwest down to the southeast, where they occupy that corner of the state. Tallgrass prairies cover most of the western state. A small region in the northwest has a mix of tallgrass prairie and aspen woods.

Woods and clouds are reflected on the surface of this beautiful lake in the mixed-forest region of Northern Minnesota.

Minnesota Borders

North:	Canada
South:	Iowa
East:	Wisconsin Lake Superior
West:	North Dakota South Dakota

Mixed Forests

Mixed forests, with pine, aspen, and birch trees, blanket northeastern Minnesota. This area is shaped like an arrowhead, with Canada to the north and Lake Superior to the south and east. It is the snowiest part of the state. Minnesota's tallest peak, Eagle Mountain, is located here. It rises 2,301 feet (701 m) above sea level. Lake Superior makes up 150 miles (240 kilometers) of the area's varied shoreline. Boaters on the beautiful lake can see waterfalls tumbling down cliffs some 1,000 feet (300 m) high. Through the port of Duluth on Lake Superior, Minnesota is connected to the other four Great Lakes, to the St. Lawrence River, and finally to the Atlantic Ocean.

The Arrowhead area is famous for its Boundary Waters Canoe Area Wilderness, which straddles the border with Canada. Here, more than 1,000 lakes and streams cut through lush forests. People can travel for hours in nonmotorized boats, stopping to fish or simply to enjoy the area's peaceful beauty.

Northern Minnesota includes the northernmost point in the United States outside Alaska. This "point" is actually within a huge lake called Lake of the Woods. The town of Angle Inlet is located on a section of Minnesota land that juts into Lake of the Woods. It is the northernmost town in the lower 48 states.

The region also includes the Mesabi Range, where rocky hills zigzag 130 miles (210 km) from south of Ely to Grand Rapids. The range gets its name from an Ojibwe legend about a red giant named Mesabe who slept in the earth. In 1887, a miner discovered iron ore in the range, and Minnesota soon became one of America's key iron-mining states.

North-central Minnesota also has mixed forests of evergreen and deciduous trees. In addition, this area has many lakes and large areas of wetlands. The source of the Mississippi River is located in this region. People come long distances to Minnesota's oldest state park, Itasca State Park, to walk across the mighty river at its source. From there, the Mississippi travels south about 2,340 miles (3,765 km) to reach the Gulf of Mexico. Starting as a trickle, the waters of the Mississippi grow into the largest river in North America in terms of volume of water carried.

A family canoes on Poplar Lake in the Boundary Waters Canoe Area Wilderness.

MINNESOTA
POPULATION BY COUNTY

County	Population	County	Population	County	Population
Aitkin County	16,202	Lake of the Woods County	4,045	Todd County	24,895
Anoka County	330,844	Le Sueur County	27,703	Traverse County	3,558
Becker County	32,504	Lincoln County	5,896	Wabasha County	21,676
Beltrami County	44,442	Lyon County	25,857	Wadena County	13,843
Benton County	38,451	Mahnomen County	5,413	Waseca County	19,136
Big Stone County	5,269	Marshall County	9,439	Washington County	238,136
Blue Earth County	64,013	Martin County	20,840	Watonwan County	11,211
Brown County	25,893	McLeod County	36,651	Wilkin County	6,576
Carlton County	35,386	Meeker County	23,300	Winona County	51,461
Carver County	91,042	Mille Lacs County	26,097	Wright County	124,700
Cass County	28,567	Morrison County	33,198	Yellow Medicine County	10,438
Chippewa County	12,441	Mower County	39,163		
Chisago County	53,887	Murray County	8,725		
Clay County	58,999	Nicollet County	32,727		
Clearwater County	8,695	Nobles County	21,378		
Cook County	5,176	Norman County	6,852		
Cottonwood County	11,687	Olmsted County	144,248		
Crow Wing County	62,500	Otter Tail County	57,303		
Dakota County	398,552	Pennington County	13,930		
Dodge County	20,087	Pine County	29,750		
Douglas County	36,009	Pipestone County	9,596		
Faribault County	14,553	Polk County	31,600		
Fillmore County	20,866	Pope County	10,995		
Freeborn County	31,255	Ramsey County	508,640		
Goodhue County	46,183	Red Lake County	4,089		
Grant County	6,018	Redwood County	16,059		
Hennepin County	1,152,425	Renville County	15,730		
Houston County	19,027	Rice County	64,142		
Hubbard County	20,428	Rock County	9,687		
Isanti County	37,816	Roseau County	15,629		
Itasca County	45,058	St. Louis County	200,226		
Jackson County	10,266	Scott County	129,928		
Kanabec County	16,239	Sherburne County	88,499		
Kandiyohi County	42,239	Sibley County	15,226		
Kittson County	4,552	Stearns County	150,642		
Koochiching County	13,311	Steele County	36,576		
Lac qui Parle County	7,259	Stevens County	9,726		
Lake County	10,866	Swift County	9,783		

Source: U.S. Bureau of the Census, 2010

Cook County

Ramsey County

The scenic Saint Croix, one of the state's major rivers, flows along the Minnesota-Wisconsin border before finally emptying into the Mississippi.

Deciduous Forests

In the southeast and a band extending diagonally across the rest of the state is a region of deciduous forests that include maple, ash, oak, and elm trees. The region has open woods and scattered prairies. The Saint Croix, Minnesota, and other large rivers have cut deep valleys through the landscape. They give Minnesota some of its most dramatic scenery.

The southeastern corner of Minnesota has rolling, forest-covered hills cut by deep streams that rush down to join the Mississippi River. Drier hillsides are covered with waving grasses. The last set of glaciers from the north did not scrape across this area of Minnesota. That is why it is much more rugged than the rest of the state.

Western Prairies

Western Minnesota is generally drier than eastern parts of the state. For this reason, prairies (grasslands) rather than forests are the main ecosystem. About 10,000 years ago, this area was at the bottom of part of a huge lake called Lake Agassiz, which formed as the glaciers melted. After the lake drained away a few thousand years later, the deepest part of the lake became a flat, fertile plain. Today, the Red River flows across this region. The Red River Valley is known for its oats, corn, and bright yellow sunflowers.

Aspen Woods and Prairies

The aspen woods and prairies in part of northern Minnesota make up the smallest of the state's natural regions. This region forms a transition between the mixed forests to the east and the tallgrass prairies to the west. The area also was once covered by Lake Agassiz. However, the lake was shallower here than it was to the west, and the lake bottom was made up mainly of sand or rocks. So the soil today is less fertile, and less of the prairie has been converted to farmland.

The Climate

Minnesotans joke that their state's climate is "ten months of winter and two months of rough sledding." Snow covers much of the state from mid-December to mid-March. The snowiest part of Minnesota, along Lake Superior, gets close to 6 feet (almost 2 m) of snow every winter. Even the drier southwestern region averages 3 feet (almost 1 m) of snow yearly. And with Minnesota's cold winters, the snow sticks around. In Minneapolis, which is in the southern part of the state, January temperatures average 13 degrees Fahrenheit (−10.6 degrees Celsius), and the average winter has 30 days when the temperature falls to 0 °F (−18 °C) or lower. Places in northern Minnesota have from time to time reported winter temperatures close to −40 °F (−40 °C). There is no question about it: Minnesotans need plenty of warm clothes because the state gets very cold and snowy in the winter.

Maples, birches, and other deciduous trees show off their fall colors as they spread over rolling hills in the southeastern part of the state.

★ 10 KEY SITES ★ ★ ★

Como Conservatory

Mall of America

Minneapolis Institute of Arts

1. Como Park Zoo and Conservatory

Located in Como Park, in St. Paul, the zoo features arctic foxes, flamingos, cougars, and zebras. The **conservatory** has gardens and many exotic plants. Visitors can also enjoy a carousel, athletic fields, miniature golf, and picnic areas.

2. Fort Snelling

Fort Snelling sits at the confluence, or junction, of the Mississippi and Minnesota rivers. It was built in 1819 to protect the area in the midst of the fur trade and the ending of the War of 1812. Today, visitors can tour the fort and learn about its history.

3. Mall of America

The Mall of America, in Bloomington, is one of the largest malls in the world. The mall features more than 500 stores, a theme park, an aquarium, and a miniature golf course. More than 40 million people visit the Mall of America each year.

4. Mill City Museum

Located on the Mississippi River in Minneapolis, the Mill City Museum was built into the ruins of what was once the world's largest flour mill. Visitors learn about the history of the flour industry, the river, and the city of Minneapolis.

5. Minneapolis Institute of Arts

This 8-acre (3.2-hectar) fine art museum features more than 80,000 objects that include paintings, photographs, sculptures, architecture, prints, and textiles from all over the world.

MINNESOTA ★ ★ ★ ★

6. Minneapolis Sculpture Garden

This 11-acre (4.5-ha) site located near the Walker Art Center features more than 40 works of art. Visitors enjoy sculptures and seasonal displays in the Cowles Conservatory and the Alene Grossman Memorial Arbor and Flower Garden.

7. Minnehaha Park

More than 850,000 visitors visit this Minneapolis park each year. The 193-acre (78-ha) park features a 53-foot (16-m) waterfall and river overlooks. Visitors can walk, bike, have picnics, and see concerts there as well.

8. Science Museum of Minnesota

The Science Museum of Minnesota focuses on physical science, natural history, and technology. Permanent exhibits include the Dinosaurs and Fossils Gallery, Big Back Yard, Human Body Gallery, and an Experiment Gallery.

9. Sea Life Minnesota Aquarium

Located at the Mall of America, in Bloomington, the Sea Life Aquarium is the largest underground aquarium in the world. It is home to more than 10,000 creatures, including sharks, stingrays, sea turtles, and different types of fish.

10. Superior National Forest

Located in Northeast Minnesota, the Superior National Forest is more than 3,900,000 acres (1,578,274 ha) of woods and water. Visitors to the park take advantage of its beauty through camping, hiking, fishing, and boating.

Minneapolis Sculpture Garden

Minnehaha Park

Science Museum of Minnesota

Snow blankets a Minnesota prairie. Winter in the state can be brutally cold.

Weather Records

The coldest temperature ever recorded in Minnesota was -60 °F [-51 °C], which was reached near the town of Tower on February 2, 1996. The record for the most snowfall during a 24-hour period was 36 inches [91 cm] on January 7, 1994, near Finland.

In Minnesota's larger cities, people use skyways—enclosed, aboveground walkways between buildings—to avoid the cold. At night, some Minnesotans plug their cars into electric warmers to keep the engines from freezing. But for those who love winter sports, Minnesota is a paradise. Snow-covered hills are great for sledding and downhill skiing. Forest paths are used for cross-country skiing and snowmobiling. Frozen lakes provide places to skate and play hockey. When the ice gets thick enough, many Minnesotans walk out on the surface and go fishing. They cut holes in the ice to drop in fishing lines. When the ice gets really thick, some people even drive onto the lake and set up an ice-fishing shack—a hut or other shelter to block the wind. They can often leave the shelter up for much of the winter.

Summer may come as a relief to many Minnesotans, but it is not always a reward. Normal July temperatures in Minneapolis range from about 63 °F to 83 °F (17 °C to 28 °C), but it can get hotter than that. The temperature in Minneapolis has gone as high as 105 °F (40.5 °C). In Moorhead on July 6, 1936, the temperature reached a record high for the state, hitting 114 °F (46 °C). Minnesotans who prefer cooler weather can head to the shores of Lake Superior during the summer. The surface of the massive lake acts like a giant air conditioner, cooling the air above it, which then blows onshore and cools shore areas to comfortable levels.

Wildlife

Minnesota's different ecosystems allow for a wide variety of plants and animals. Bluestem grasses, blazingstar flowers, black-eyed Susans, and prairie smoke flowers are among the many colorful plants that brighten the prairie. Trees add year-round interest. Aspen trees are common in the deciduous and mixed forests. In summer, their leaves shimmer in the breeze. Maple trees grow in many parts of the state. In the fall, their leaves turn beautiful shades of orange, red, and yellow. Pine, spruce, and other evergreen trees dominate parts of northern and eastern Minnesota. In the winter, they add dark beauty to the snow-covered Minnesota landscape.

Aspen trees are common in Minnesota's forests. The tree's wood is soft and is often used to make paper and matches.

White-tailed deer are commonly found in Minnesota's woodland areas and prairies.

The fields and forests are also home to deer, beavers, raccoons, and squirrels. In the woods, you may see skunks, martens, porcupines, and red and gray foxes. The howls of wolves and coyote often pierce the night. Larger animals include moose, elk, and black bears.

Minnesota has a large bird population. Common songbirds such as robins, cardinals, goldfinches, and many others nest in the state. Water-loving species, including Canada geese, mallards, and wood ducks, also abound. In addition, the state lies at the northern edge of the Mississippi flyway, a long **migration** route taken by birds as they travel to and from their winter homes farther south. About 100 species of birds migrate through Minnesota every year. There may be hundreds of thousands of birds flying through at any given time.

However, some birds that had been very common in Minnesota have begun to drop in numbers. For example, eastern meadowlarks, red-headed woodpeckers, and northern pintail ducks all are on the decline. Scientists think these birds have fewer good places to find food and to nest because more people now settle or vacation on grasslands, in woods, and along waterways. Minnesotans are working to keep wild lands wild. They also plant native species of flowers, trees, and shrubs in their yards and parks to help attract birds.

Aquatic, or water-loving, animals thrive in Minnesota. Several types of salamanders, frogs, snakes, and turtles live in and around the state's waterways. Minnesota's waters are home to many fish species, and the state has a big sports fishing industry. Minnesota sells more fishing licenses for the size of its population than any other state. Among the most popular fish are walleye, northern pike, bass, and muskie.

Preservation and Protection

Federal, state, and local governments work together with residents to preserve and protect Minnesota's wildlife. Hunting is limited by state regulation. Laws have been passed to prevent people from killing protected animals or disturbing the habitats of animals that are threatened or **endangered**. Minnesota's plant life is also protected. It is illegal to pick any plants that the government has listed as endangered or threatened.

Minnesotans have also worked on their own to help preserve the state's natural environment. An example is the Minnesota Conservation Corps (MCC), which was started by the state legislature in 1981 and now operates without state funding. Through this organization, young people take on jobs involving such tasks as building trails and log shelters, improving campgrounds, and keeping track of how well different kinds of animals are surviving in the wild.

Canada geese are among the many water-loving birds that make their home in the state.

10 KEY PLANTS AND ANIMALS

Badger

Gray Wolf

Monarch Butterfly

1. Badger

A badger is a mammal that has a short, fat body and short legs. It has brown or black fur with white stripes on its cheeks and a stripe running from its nose to its head. Badgers live in fields, farmland, and along the edges of woods.

2. State Bird: Common Loon

Loons have black heads and necks, red eyes, and white stripes and spots. They grow up to three feet (91 cm) long, and they weigh up to 12 pounds (5 kg). The loon's call is a wail, and it can be heard at great distances.

3. Gray Wolf

Despite their name, not all gray wolves are gray. Some have tan, reddish, brown, or black fur. Gray wolves usually hunt in packs of six to twelve. There are a few thousand gray wolves in Minnesota. They are at risk of becoming endangered and thus possibly extinct.

4. State Mushroom: Morel

These brown, spongy-topped mushrooms add an unusual flavor to many foods. Each spring, expert mushroom hunters search Minnesota's fields and forests for morels. But they have to watch out, because mushrooms that look a lot like morels may be poisonous.

5. State Butterfly: Monarch

Minnesota is home to more than 100 different types of butterflies. Monarch butterflies travel to a warmer place for the winter. After spending the summer in Minnesota, they fly south all the way to central Mexico. Their journey takes several months and covers some 1,800 miles (3,000 km).

MINNESOTA

6. Moose

Moose can weigh more than 1,000 pounds (450 kg). Their long legs and the shape of their hooves help them move easily in marshy areas and along lakes and streams. Their numbers have been falling greatly. Many scientists believe warmer weather is partly to blame.

7. State Tree: Norway Pine

The Norway pine became Minnesota's State Tree in 1953. Norway pines grow up to 80 feet (24 m) tall and 36 inches (91 cm) in diameter. The tree is often used for timber, so more Norway pines have been planted in Minnesota than any other tree.

8. State Flower: Pink and White Lady's Slipper

The lady's slipper has been the State Flower since 1902. Its pink and white petals are the reason the lady's slipper is considered one of the most beautiful flowers in the state. However, its leaves can cause a rash on some people.

9. State Fish: Walleye

Big, marblelike eyes with white pupils give this fish its name. The walleye is important to the state's huge sports fishing industry. Most walleyes caught and kept in Minnesota weigh just over a pound (0.5 kg). But the largest walleye caught in the state weighed more than 17 pounds, 8 ounces (almost 8 kg).

10. State Grain: Wild Rice

Wild rice can be found in shallow bodies of water mainly in northern and central Minnesota. Native Americans who lived in the area many hundreds of years ago harvested and ate the rice. Minnesotans still harvest wild rice today.

Moose

Lady's Slipper

Walleye

This illustration depicts members of the Ojibwe tribe performing a war dance.

From the Beginning

Thousands of years ago, migrants crossed from Asia into North America. Some traveled across a northern land bridge that once connected Siberia and Alaska. In time, these early peoples spread throughout North America, eventually reaching the region that is now Minnesota.

Early Minnesotans

Before the arrival of Europeans, generation after generation of Native Americans in the region gathered plants, fished, and hunted wild animals for food and clothing. They learned to carve stone and bone and later to shape copper into tools. To honor their dead, later groups started burying them in huge mounds made of earth. Some of these mounds are still visible today. One of the largest is Grand Mound, near International Falls. It is 100 feet (30 m) long and 45 feet (14 m) tall.

By 1000 BCE the land had features similar to those of today. Forests dominated the northern and eastern parts of Minnesota and prairies were established in the west. Native peoples in the prairies developed a lifestyle centered on hunting deer and bison (commonly called buffalo). Groups that spent more time in and around forests and lakes developed a lifestyle based on fishing.

In a diorama at the Pipestone National Monument, Native Americans of the past are shown mining red stone. Continuing a long cultural tradition, Minnesota Native Americans use this red stone today to create handmade pipes in many styles and designs.

Over time, these different lifestyles became more complex. Groups that hunted on the prairies started to harvest wild rice. They found ways to store the rice by roasting it, so as to have more food to eat in the winter months. Groups that spent more time in and around the forests planted squash seeds in the fertile soil of the river valleys. They also began raising corn and beans, which could be prepared for winter storage. These changes helped both groups flourish.

Agriculture based on corn and beans became very important to Native Americans living in what is now southern Minnesota. They built large, permanent villages near their gardens. They also went on trips north to hunt, fish, and gather wild foods.

By the time the first Europeans arrived in North America, Native Americans in what is now Minnesota had been following the same cultural patterns for centuries. There were several major groups. The Ioway, who were closely related to the Winnebago in Wisconsin, lived in the river valleys of the southeast. The Dakota lived where the prairies and forests came together in north-central Minnesota. The Europeans called these people Sioux—which means "snake" and implies "enemy." The Dakota were related to the Assiniboine, who lived in northwestern Minnesota. Another group, the Cheyenne, lived just north of the Dakota, along the Upper Mississippi River.

The Europeans soon started trading with tribes. The Native Americans provided animal furs, which were very popular in Europe for coats and hats, in exchange for strong, durable tools, pots, and weapons made of iron. This trade was profitable for both groups. But it led to fierce competition among Native American tribes as well as among the European nations.

By 1660, many tribes in the East were pushing westward into the area. One of their main goals was to expand their fur-hunting grounds. They came into conflict with the tribes already living there. As the fur trade grew, more tribes became involved, and conflicts intensified. By the 1680s, the Ioway had been pushed out of what is now Minnesota. The Dakota were under pressure from the Ojibwe, who had come into the region from the area north and east of Lake Superior.

The Ojibwe had a lifestyle fairly similar to that of the Dakota. One difference was their beautiful, light birchbark canoes. The Dakota, in contrast, made their canoes from hollowed-out logs.

This picture, by the artist Frederic Remington, depicts a friendly handshake between a fur trader and a Native American leader. The fur trade benefitted both sides but led to bitter competition among tribes.

The Native People

The first Europeans to arrive in Minnesota were French fur traders, who explored the state in the early 1600s. However, groups of people had already been living in the state for millennia, practicing their unique cultures. These Native Americans were members of two distinct tribes: the Dakota Sioux and the Ojibwe, who were also called the Chippewa. The Dakota Sioux occupied the southwestern part of Minnesota, while the Ojibwe lived in the northeast.

Despite their distinct cultures and languages, the Native American tribes of Minnesota shared many similarities. They lived in wigwams, which were built using wooden frames covered in animal hides and bark. When the Native Americans moved to a new location, they would roll the hides and leave the frame. If they returned to the same spot, they could use the original frame. They fished and hunted wild game using bows, arrows, and snares. They also harvested wild rice and vegetables, such as squash and corn, and made sugar and maple syrup. Skilled artisans, they were particularly known for their beadwork. They made wampum belts out of white and purple shell beads. These belts often told a story or represented a person's family. They also crafted canoes, which they used for traveling and fishing.

Although the Natives of Minnesota, like all other Native people in North America, were removed from their lands, they generally fared better than tribes in other territories. The Ojibwe were members of a powerful, longstanding alliance with two other tribes from the Great Lakes region of the U.S. and Canada called the Council of Three Fires. This alliance was able to resist encroachment by both other Native groups and, to a large extent, Europeans. The Ojibwe were never relocated to Oklahoma and Kansas like many other tribes, and today nearly all Ojibwe reservations are located within their original territory.

There are eleven Native American tribes in Minnesota that are currently recognized by the U.S. government. These include the Bois Forte Band of Chippewa, Fond Du Lac Reservation, Grand Portage Band of Chippewa Indians, Leech Lake Band of Ojibwe, Lower Sioux Indian Community, Mille Lacs Band of Ojibwe, Prairie Island Indian Community, Red Lake Band of Chippewa Indians, Shakopee Mdewakanton Sioux Community, Upper Sioux Community, and White Earth Reservation.

Spotlight on the Ojibwe

Many believe the Ojibwe (also known as the Chippewa) spread throughout the region in the 1500s and 1600s. Historians think the name "Ojibwe" refers to either a type

This illustration depicts an Ojibwe wigwam and family on the shore of one of Minnesota's lakes.

of moccasin the Ojibwe wore or their **custom** of writing on the bark of birch trees. **Archaeologists** believe the Ojibwe traveled east along the Great Lakes in search of food, and settled in the northern part of what is now Minnesota.

Organization: Ojibwe communities were based on clans, which determined a member's place in the Ojibwe society. Different clans represented different parts of their society. Warriors were generally from the bear, lynx, or wolf clans. Political leaders came from the loon or crane clans.

Maple Syrup: The Ojibwe made maple sugar and syrup. Traditionally, women did the sugar-making. From February to April, sap ran freely in the sugar maple trees. Every day during this time, the women gathered sap and carried it to a special wigwam where it was processed. The Ojibwe then made either syrup, sugar, or cake.

Clothing: Ojibwe women wore long dresses. Ojibwe men wore breechcloths and leggings. Both men and women wore moccasins on their feet. In later years, the tribe wore clothing made from **imported** cloth they had traded with the Europeans.

Transportation: The Ojibwe were well-known for their canoes that they made out of birch bark. The tribe used canoes to travel along waterways and to fish for food.

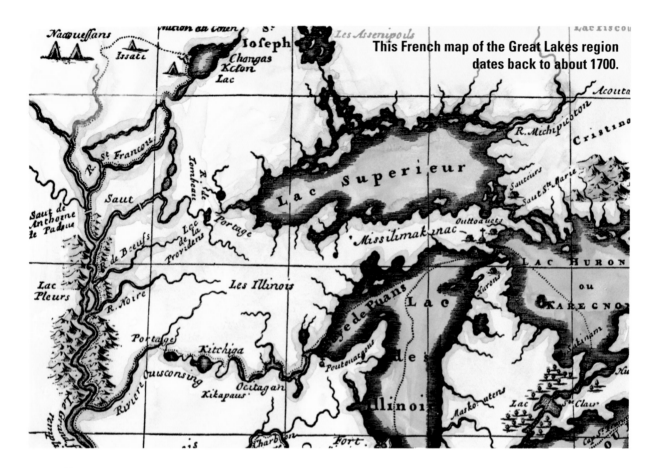

This French map of the Great Lakes region dates back to about 1700.

The Dakota and the Ojibwe had shared hunting grounds for decades, but competition over the fur trade made them bitter enemies. As the Ojibwe settled onto Dakota lands, the Dakota were gradually forced out of the northern half of what is now Minnesota.

French Explorers Arrive

The French set up fur-trading posts in eastern Canada in the early 1600s and explored many parts of North America. The first Europeans to explore the area that is now Minnesota were the French fur traders Pierre Radisson and Médard Chouart, whose title was sieur des Groseilliers. In 1660, Radisson and Groseilliers traveled through this region in search of the Northwest Passage—a water route linking the Atlantic and Pacific oceans. They did not find it (it was not there to be found). What they found instead were deep forests and abundant waterways.

In 1679, Daniel Greysolon, sieur Du Lhut (also spelled Duluth), began a long journey through the area on behalf of France. He worked to make peace among warring Native American tribes, hoping this would benefit the French fur trade. Du Lhut helped strengthen French control over the area that is now Minnesota. Years later, the city of Duluth was named after him. Another well-known figure was the French explorer and **missionary** Father Louis Hennepin. One of the state's counties is named after him.

In the next century, French traders traveled throughout the region. They soon came into conflict with the British, who competed to build a fur-trading empire in North America. By 1754, the competition between Britain and France had erupted into the French and Indian War. This conflict, which also involved Native American tribes, ended in defeat for France in 1763. Under the treaty ending the war, Britain officially gained control of virtually all the land that France had claimed in North America east of the Mississippi River, including present-day eastern Minnesota. Eventually, most of the French moved from this area. But the French names of many places in Minnesota, including such towns as Elysian, Cloquet, and Belle Plaine, indicate the importance of the French in the region's history.

Father Louis Hennepin, an early French explorer, is shown at the door of a Native American dwelling in Minnesota.

Making a Snow Globe

Snow is a part of everyday life during Minnesota's winters. Whether you are snowed in or you just want to have some fun, follow these directions to create your very own snow globe! Choose an old toy or even part of a holiday ornament to put inside it.

What You Need

Small baby food jar with lid

Hot glue gun

Small toys or ornaments that fit into the jar

Water

Gold or silver glitter

What To Do

- Have an adult help you with this step. Use a hot glue gun to glue ornaments or small toys to the inside of a baby food jar lid.
- Allow it to dry.
- Once dry, fill the jar with water.
- Sprinkle the glitter inside it.
- Place the lid on the jar tightly.
- Shake the jar and watch it snow!

The Road to Statehood

In 1775, the American colonists began their successful war for independence from Great Britain. Under a peace treaty with Britain that officially ended the American Revolution in 1783, the new United States gained control of lands east of the Mississippi River, including present-day eastern Minnesota. Twenty years later, in 1803, the United States bought the Louisiana Territory from France. This action—known as the Louisiana Purchase—added to the United States a huge area west of the Mississippi River, including the rest of what became the state of Minnesota.

In the early 1800s, the United States purchased from the Dakota an important parcel of land along the Mississippi River. It included Saint Anthony Falls and the strategic spot where the Minnesota River joins the Mississippi. The United States Army arrived at the spot in 1819 and, under the command of Colonel Josiah Snelling, built a fort there. The sturdy outpost was named Fort Saint Anthony, after the nearby waterfalls. After Snelling's death, the fort was renamed in his honor.

The area had long been a trading spot for Native Americans, many of them loyal to the British in Canada. After Fort Snelling was built, European-American settlers began arriving. Some were families of people involved in the fur trade. A group of refugees from a failed settlement in Canada were among the first permanent settlers of European heritage. The fort had the region's earliest post office, school, and hospital. It also had a flour mill and a lumber mill. In time, the settlements in the area grew into the cities of Minneapolis and St. Paul.

Did You Know?

Some items that were invented in Minnesota include Scotch tape, Wheaties cereal, the bundt pan, and Bisquick pancake mix.

This growth was slow at first. The region was remote and was very cold and isolated in winter. There was no mail service or outside trade for close to half the year. But the area had many resources, including forests rich with timber. Much of the land was Native American territory, but the U.S. government continued to pressure the Dakota and Ojibwe to give up land. Treaties signed by the Ojibwe in 1851 required most of them to leave their forests in the upper half of the region. The Dakota sold all their land east of the Red River; in return, they received only a small strip of land along the Minnesota River.

Minnesota was a land of opportunity for early settlers like this farmer, shown in the field with his oxen-drawn plow.

With the Native Americans relocated, settlers felt safer moving to the region. Steamboat travel to the area increased. Many steamboats landed at a dock near Fort Snelling known as Pig's Eye Landing. In the early 1840s, a Roman Catholic missionary built a small church nearby, dedicated to St. Paul, and Pig's Eye Landing developed into a booming port settlement. It was named St. Paul, after the mission church.

Between 1853 and 1857, the region's population grew from 40,000 to 150,000 people. The area was large enough to be granted statehood. In 1858, Minnesota became the thirty-second state. St. Paul was chosen as the capital.

Growing Pains

The new state continued to grow into the 1860s. Small farms sprouted on the plains. Villages sprang up along waterways. The telegraph connected distant towns. The U.S. government offered money to build a network of railroads. To find workers, railroad companies arranged to have steamship lines bring European **immigrants** into Minnesota.

Around the same time, the U.S. government passed a law (known as the Homestead Act) granting 160 acres (65 hectares) of land in the American Midwest or Far West to anyone who agreed to build and live on the land for five years. Many immigrants came to

Minnesota from western and northern Europe, especially Sweden, Norway, and Germany. They were eager to own land and start farms in the new state.

From 1861 to 1865, the Civil War raged between the Northern (Union) and Southern (Confederate) states. Minnesota sent almost 24,000 soldiers to fight in Union armies. (The Union's victory in 1865 resulted in the end of slavery in the United States.)

Meanwhile, a different battle raged on Minnesota soil, between the Dakota and the settlers. The U.S. government rarely kept its treaty promises, and the Dakota got little in return for lands they had sold. As their lands shrank, they grew hungrier and angrier. Then, on August 17, 1862, a small band of Dakota attacked settlers near Acton. Three white men and two women died.

At first, Dakota chief Taoyateduta, or Little Crow, tried to keep peace. But other Dakota believed this was a good time to chase out the settlers, since so many men were off fighting in the Civil War. So Dakota warriors attacked farms and forts and burned buildings. Former governor Henry Sibley led a group of soldiers against the Dakota. By the time the Native Americans surrendered near the end of September, more than 400 settlers had been killed. The army rounded up 1,700 Dakota, including women, children, and elders as well as warriors. The warriors were put on trial and more than 300 were sentenced to death. President Abraham Lincoln reduced most of the sentences to prison terms, but he upheld the **execution** of 38 Dakota people. This was the biggest mass execution in U.S. history.

Children were expected to help out with everyday tasks on the family farm.

10 KEY CITIES

Minneapolis

St. Paul

Duluth

1. Minneapolis: population 382,578

Minneapolis, the largest city in Minnesota, is often called the "City of Lakes." The area includes 20 lakes and wetlands, creeks, and the Mississippi River. It is the primary business center between Chicago and Seattle.

2. St. Paul: population 285,068

St. Paul is the capital of Minnesota. It is located just east of Minneapolis. These two cities are known as the "Twin Cities." The Minneapolis-St. Paul area is the sixteenth-largest metropolitan area in the United States.

3. Rochester: population 106,769

Rochester, southeast of Minneapolis, was named a "Best Small City" by *Money* magazine. It said, "One thing to remember about Rochester is that it has the sophistication of a larger metro area, but not the congestion or the complications."

4. Duluth: population 86,265

Duluth sits on the shore of Lake Superior, making it a popular place for people to visit. The city has theater, concerts, and shopping. Duluth is frequently ranked as one of the best and most affordable places to live in America.

5. Bloomington: population 82,893

Located on the banks of the Minnesota River, Bloomington is home to the famous Mall of America. The city also has the Minnesota Valley National Wildlife Refuge, Water Park of America, and hiking and biking trails.

MINNESOTA

6. Brooklyn Park: population 75,781

Located along the Mississippi River, Brooklyn Park features around 2,000 acres (809 ha) of parks, several golf courses, and 120 miles (193 km) of trails. Many people who work in the Minneapolis-St. Paul area live in this quiet suburb.

7. Plymouth: population 70,576

A suburb of Minneapolis, Plymouth offers lakes, trails, good school districts, and quiet neighborhoods. The city has been ranked twice on *Money* magazine's list of "America's Best Places to Live."

8. St. Cloud: population 65,842

St. Cloud calls itself the economic, social, and cultural heart of the state. It is a community with deep roots in agriculture and granite. The area features the latest in health care, education, and technology.

9. Eagan: population 64,206

Eagan is a popular place to live because of its proximity to the airport, highways, and other Twin Cities conveniences. In 2012, *Money* magazine ranked it as the fourteenth best place to live in the United States.

10. Woodbury: population 61,961

Woodbury, just outside St. Paul, features 3,000 acres (1,214 ha) of park land, 40 community and neighborhood parks, and a swimming beach. The city is home to some major companies, including The Hartford and Target.com.

Brooklyn Park

Eagan

Loggers from the 1890s carry timber through the forest on a sled pulled by oxen.

Farmers, Loggers, and Miners

In the mid–1860s, Minnesota started a period of rapid growth. Land was cleared for farming in much of the southern, central, and western regions. The settlers suffered many hardships, including **plagues** of grasshoppers that destroyed their crops. But they worked hard to build a new life for themselves in this new land. By 1878, wheat, Minnesota's main crop, filled about 70 percent of the state's fields. This was good for the flour-milling industry in Minneapolis. In fact, the city had become known as the flour-milling capital of the world.

The logging industry started in central Minnesota in the mid–1800s. At first, Native Americans were the region's main lumberjacks. They cut down trees and sent them downriver to lumber mills. As loggers cleared more land, they moved farther north. The logging industry in Minnesota reached its peak around 1900. Owners of lumber companies became rich. But they had cut down most of the state's white pines, and, in all, one-third of Minnesota's forests were gone.

In the late 1880s, a miner working for the Merritt family discovered a big deposit of iron in the Mesabi Range. Unlike other finds, this rich ore lay near the surface and was easy to reach. The first mine soon opened, and in time, Minnesota was supplying almost three-fourths of the nation's iron ore. Steel-making also became an important industry in the state. In 1916, U.S. Steel—one of the largest steel companies at the time—opened a steel mill near Duluth. It remained in operation for more than 60 years.

Iron mines in Minnesota's Mesabi Range contributed to the state's economic development and population growth in the late 1800s and beyond.

This illustration depicts a speaker talking to farmers at an early Grange meeting.

Workers Speak Out

Big companies took over many Minnesota industries, including mining, food processing, and manufacturing industries, as well as railroads. Factory workers often were paid low wages and struggled to make a decent living. But the first major call for change came from farmers. Besides the risk of bad weather and years of low prices for their crops, the farmers had to pay high rates to store their crops in giant towers called grain elevators. They also paid heavily to ship their crops to market by rail. They needed a way to reduce costs.

In 1867, a Minnesota farmer named Oliver H. Kelley began a group called the Grange to fight for the rights of the farmers. It spread rapidly throughout Minnesota and other farm states. Members bought equipment and supplies as a group in order to lower costs. They also elected people to government offices who would pass laws to help farmers. These laws, called the Grange Acts, limited the fees railroad and grain elevator owners could charge farmers.

The Grange helped farmers throughout the country gain political and economic power.

Among other workers, iron miners banded together to seek, and sometimes go on strike for, better working conditions and pay. Walkouts also occurred among loggers and sawmill workers. Companies often responded by hiring men to break up the workers' organizations (labor unions) and force the workers to give up their protests.

Minnesota's most famous strike came when Minneapolis truckers walked off the job, calling for companies to recognize their union. The climax came on July 20, 1934, when police fired into a group of unarmed strikers. A few of the strikers died, and some 200 were wounded. The day became known as Bloody Friday. The event helped build support for labor unions, not only in Minnesota but in the rest of the country as well.

Heavy Traffic

Logjams were common along the state's waterways. The worst was recorded in 1889. Logs backed up a 2.5-mile-long [4-km-long] stretch of the Saint Croix River; the pileup of logs was 100 feet [30 m] deep.

Fighting breaks out during the trucker strike of 1934.

Like many Minnesotans, this poor farm family, from Hollandale, suffered hardships during the Great Depression.

That's a Lot of Twine

For many years, one of the world's largest balls of twine has sat in Darwin. It weighs 17,400 pounds [7,893 kg], is 12 feet [3.7 m] in diameter, and was the creation of Francis A. Johnson.

Hard Times

By this time, the Great Depression was in full swing, and life was hard for workers throughout the country. In Minnesota, large numbers of factory workers and miners lost their jobs. Farmers were also affected by the hard times. Grain prices fell, and some farmers could not afford to plant new crops. In 1932, farmers called a strike to get higher prices for their crops. They blocked roads to prevent food from being delivered to big-city markets. A year later, they marched to the State Capitol in St. Paul. This time, they helped get a law passed to block banks from taking farms away from families who owed money and could not repay their loans.

World War II (in which the United States fought from 1941 to 1945) helped end the Depression in Minnesota and the rest of the nation. Farmers produced food for soldiers, and iron was needed for military equipment. Another milestone came in 1959, when the St. Lawrence Seaway opened. It allowed big ships from the Atlantic Ocean to sail all the way to Duluth at the western end of the Great Lakes, giving Minnesota's mines and other industries an international port.

A view of the St. Lawrence Seaway in 1958, a year before its opening.

Modern Minnesota

Minnesotans have a strong tradition of thinking independently and speaking out to express their views. Minnesota's own political party, the Farmer-Labor Party, was the most powerful party in the state during the early 1900s. After it merged with the Democratic Party in 1944, the Democratic-Farmer-Labor Party (DFL) continued to produce influential political leaders, especially in the U.S. Senate. Minnesotans also showed their independence in 1998 when they elected Jesse "The Body" Ventura governor of Minnesota. Ventura was best known as a professional wrestler, sports commentator, and actor.

Along with the rest of the nation, Minnesota suffered from a recession, or downturn in the economy, that began at the end of 2007 and then became more severe. From mid–2008 to mid–2009, the state lost more than 100,000 jobs. However, the unemployment rate, or percentage of workers who were out of work and looking for a job, was still lower than the average for the United States as a whole.

Minnesota continues to be a place where people come first. As author and radio personality Garrison Keillor wrote, Minnesota "produces good-hearted people who are tolerant, helpful, and friendly."

Today, Minnesota's population and economy continue to grow.

10 KEY DATES IN STATE HISTORY

1. 1660

French explorers Pierre Radisson and Médard Chouart, sieur des Groseilliers, travel through what is now southeastern Minnesota.

2. 1679

Daniel Greysolon, sieur Du Lhut, visits what is now Minnesota and helps strengthen French control over the region.

3. February 10, 1763

The British win the French and Indian War, and much of present-day Minnesota comes under British control.

4. September 3, 1783

With America's victory in the American Revolution, the part of Minnesota east of the Mississippi River becomes part of the United States.

5. April 30, 1803

The United States buys the Louisiana Territory from France, including the part of Minnesota west of the Mississippi River, in the Louisiana Purchase. The U.S. pays more than $11 million.

6. May 11, 1858

The eastern half of the Minnesota Territory becomes the 32nd state. The western part remains unorganized until 1861.

7. April 25, 1959

The St. Lawrence Seaway is opened. It allows ships from the Atlantic Ocean to sail to the western end of the Great Lakes.

8. November 2, 1976

Senator Walter Mondale, another prominent Minnesotan, is elected U.S. Vice President. Jimmy Carter is elected President.

9. August 1, 2007

A highway bridge across the Mississippi River in Minneapolis collapses, killing 13 people. Another 145 people are injured in the accident.

10. May 14, 2013

Governor Mark Dayton signs a bill that legalizes same-sex marriage. It goes into effect on August 1.

A younger fisherman holds his catch.
Walleyes are Minnesota's State Fish.

The People

Through the years, the hunt for land and jobs has brought waves of people to Minnesota. Today, Minnesota still attracts newcomers, both from other states and from foreign countries. Despite the long cold winters, the state ranks high in quality of life, with its excellent schools, lively midsize cities, quiet lakes, and welcoming neighbors. Minnesotans old and new belong to different races and ethnic groups, contributing their own customs, traditions, and holidays to life in the state.

Minnesota had more than 5.3 million people in 2010, making it the twenty-first most populated state. The population has shifted in recent decades from country to city living. Almost three-fourths of Minnesotans now live in an urban area.

Around 60 percent of the population lives in the Minneapolis–St. Paul metropolitan area, which includes these two "Twin Cities" and the many smaller cities and suburbs surrounding them. Minneapolis by itself is the largest city, with an estimated population of 392,880 in 2012. Right on its border, across the Mississippi, is the city of St. Paul, the state capital. It had a population of 285,068 in 2010. Rochester, to the south, is the third-largest city (population, 106,769), and Duluth, on Lake Superior, ranks fourth, with 86,265 people as of 2010. Rochester and Duluth are the centers of their own metropolitan areas.

A German band performs at an ethnic festival in the town of New Ulm, where many German Americans keep old traditions alive.

Do I Have to Eat it?

One tradition that has survived among many of Minnesota's Scandinavian Americans is that of eating lutefisk in the winter months. This dish consists of dried whitefish soaked for a long time in lye. Not everyone finds it tasty, and it is the subject of many jokes. The town of Madison, Minnesota, calls itself the "lutefisk capital" of the United States.

But Minnesota's fifth-largest city, Bloomington (population, 82,893), is close to the Twin Cities and part of the Minneapolis–St. Paul metropolitan area. In fact, most of Minnesota's 20 biggest cities are part of that metropolitan area.

Ethnic Diversity

The face of Minnesota has changed over the years. The earliest residents were Native Americans. French-Canadian fur trappers and missionaries were the first Europeans to arrive. They were followed by people of English heritage. In the 1800s, large numbers of German, Swedish, Norwegian, Danish, and Irish people settled in different parts of the state. The late 1800s also saw new waves of immigrants from Eastern Europe, including Polish and Czech people, and from Finland.

At first, members of these different ethnic groups spoke their own languages and kept to their old customs. Entire towns, such as New Ulm and Sleepy Eye, spoke German for decades. These groups still preserve elements of their cultural heritage. But over the years, they have become less distinct, blending in with the Midwestern lifestyle.

Today, most Minnesotans are of European background. But there are also African Americans, as well as Hispanic Americans who trace their ancestry to Latin America. Many recent immigrants to Minnesota are from parts of Asia and Africa. These people continue to make the state culturally diverse.

Many immigrants came from Southeast Asia after the end of the Vietnam War in 1975. People from groups that had aided the American side feared that they were in danger from Communist governments that had gained control of the region. Among these immigrants were Hmong people from the mountains of Vietnam and Laos. Minnesota today has more Hmong people than any other state except California.

Living in Minnesota was a big change, but the Hmong and others from Southeast Asia are making progress in adjusting to their new lives. In 2002, Mee Moua was elected to the Minnesota state Senate, becoming the first-ever Hmong-American state legislator.

Minnesota also has the largest Tibetan community in the United States outside New York, and the state has attracted many immigrants from African countries. The biggest group is from Somalia. War and poverty there have forced tens of thousands to leave their homeland. Church groups and others in Minnesota have helped immigrants resettle, and the state has developed programs to meet the special needs of immigrants and of **minorities**.

Native Americans from a Minnesota reservation harvest wild rice.

★ 10 KEY PEOPLE ★

Bob Dylan

Louise Erdrich

Kris Humphries

1. Jessica Biel

Born in 1982 in Ely, Jessica Biel starred in the TV show *7th Heaven* when she was a teenager. She later appeared in the movies *Valentine's Day*, *Elizabethtown,* and *Total Recall*. She married pop star Justin Timberlake.

2. Bob Dylan

Bob Dylan was born in Duluth in 1941. During the 1960s and 1970s, his folk and rock music, with its messages calling for peace and equal rights, attracted millions of fans. In 1988, Dylan was inducted into the Rock and Roll Hall of Fame.

3. Louise Erdrich

Louise Erdrich was born in 1954 in Little Falls, and grew up in North Dakota. As a child she learned about Ojibwe traditions from her grandfather, who had been the leader of a branch of the Ojibwe. Erdrich has written more than two dozen books and has earned many awards, including the National Book Award.

4. Judy Garland

Judy Garland was born in 1922 in Grand Rapids. When she was only 13, Garland signed a movie contract. In 1939, she starred in one of the most beloved movies of all time, *The Wizard of Oz*. She continued to sing and act in many movies until her death in 1969.

5. Kris Humphries

Kris Humphries was born in Minneapolis in 1985. After playing basketball in high school, he became an impressive player on the University of Minnesota's team. He was drafted by the Utah Jazz in 2004. He has since played for the Toronto Raptors, Brooklyn Nets, and Boston Celtics.

★ MINNESOTA ★ ★ ★ ★

Sinclair Lewis

Chris Pratt

Brianna Scurry

★ 6. Sinclair Lewis

Sinclair Lewis was born in 1885 in Sauk Centre, a small Minnesota town. In *Main Street* and other widely read novels, he paints a picture of small-town life in America. In 1930, Lewis became the first American to win the Nobel Prize in Literature. He died in 1951.

★ 7. Chris Pratt

Born in Virginia, Minnesota in 1979, Chris Pratt did not plan on becoming an actor. He was discovered while waiting tables in Hawaii. Since then, Pratt has starred in the TV shows *Everwood* and *Parks and Recreation*.

★ 8. Charles Schulz

Born in Minneapolis in 1922, Schulz drew a weekly cartoon for a St. Paul newspaper before creating the famous comic strip *Peanuts*. His *Peanuts* characters have been known and loved around the world for more than 60 years.

★ 9. Brianna Scurry

Briana Scurry is an American soccer star. Born in Minneapolis in 1971, she went to the University of Massachusetts. There she starred as a goalie. During the 1990s and the early 2000s, Scurry helped the U.S. National Team gain both World Cup and Olympic victories.

★ 10. Roy Wilkins

Born in Missouri in 1901, Roy Wilkins grew up in St. Paul. He became a newspaper editor and a leader in the civil rights movement. He headed the National Association for the Advancement of Colored People (NAACP) for many years. In 1969, Wilkins received the Presidential Medal of Freedom.

Who Minnesotans Are

Total Population
5,303,925

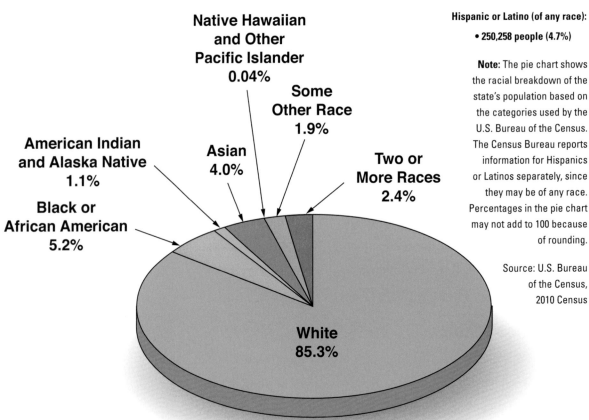

Native Hawaiian
and Other
Pacific Islander
0.04%

Some
Other Race
1.9%

American Indian
and Alaska Native
1.1%

Asian
4.0%

Two or
More Races
2.4%

Black or
African American
5.2%

White
85.3%

Hispanic or Latino (of any race):

• 250,258 people (4.7%)

Note: The pie chart shows the racial breakdown of the state's population based on the categories used by the U.S. Bureau of the Census. The Census Bureau reports information for Hispanics or Latinos separately, since they may be of any race. Percentages in the pie chart may not add to 100 because of rounding.

Source: U.S. Bureau
of the Census,
2010 Census

Most of the recent immigrants and members of minority groups in Minnesota, including African Americans and Hispanic Americans, have their largest communities in the Twin Cities. Parts of Minneapolis and St. Paul have an international flavor, with ethnic grocery stores and restaurants.

Adding to Minnesota's ethnic diversity are the more than 50,000 Ojibwe, Dakota, and other Native American residents. Many live in the Twin Cities. Some of the others live on reservations.

State Song

Minnesota's State Song is "Hail! Minnesota." It was written by Truman Elwell Rickard and Arthur Wheelock Upson.

Good Schools for Everyone

Surveys have ranked Minnesota near the top among U.S. states in providing high-quality public schools. The state also ranks near the top for the percentage of residents who have graduated from high school.

School officials and teachers have often been leaders in finding new ways to improve education. For example, in 1992 the nation's first charter school opened in the state of Minnesota. Charter schools are free public schools that are run separately from the public school system. They try new or different teaching methods and were created to help more students do well in school.

Somali students (right) work with a group during class.

A teacher works with students in a classroom in St. Paul.

In Their Own Words

"Well, my take was people of Minnesota, these are good people. They're in many ways more generous than other parts of the country. They're better educated than other parts of the country."
—Peter Agre, physician and professor

In addition, schools often have special programs devoted to the culture of particular ethnic groups, and many schools, especially in urban areas, provide classes in Spanish or certain African, Asian, or Native American languages to help meet the needs of students.

On the college level, the University of Minnesota, with campuses in the Twin Cities and four other locations, has one of the best reputations of any state university. The state also has a fine system of state colleges and many excellent private colleges, including Carleton College and St. Olaf College, in Northfield, and Macalester College in St. Paul, to name a few.

★ 10 ★ KEY EVENTS ★ ★ ★

Bavarian Blast

Icebox Days

Land of the Loon Festival

1. Bavarian Blast

The entire town of New Ulm comes alive with an old-world German festival in July. Singers trill, tubas oompah, and crowds enjoy German foods, crafts, and costumes. There is also a race and a parade.

2. Bayfront Blues Festival

One of the largest music festivals in the Midwest , the Bayfront Blues Festival features music performances on two concert stages. It attracts more than 20,000 people who gather on the banks of Lake Superior to enjoy the summer music.

3. Festival of Nations

Since 1932, St. Paul has hosted one of the nation's largest and oldest celebrations of international culture. The event, which is held in the spring, offers dance, food, and art from various countries.

4. Icebox Days

Every January, the people of International Falls celebrate the winter season. Residents and visitors can enjoy candlelight skiing, an old-fashioned bonfire, ice skating, snowshoe races, snow and ice sculptures, and the "freeze yer gizzard" blizzard run.

5. Land of the Loon Festival

In June, hundreds of Minnesotans gather in the city of Virginia to honor the State Bird. Activities include a parade, arts-and-crafts displays, food, music, and magic acts. This festival has been going strong for more than 35 years.

MINNESOTA ★ ★ ★ ★ ★

6. Lefse Dagen (Pancake Day)

In 1983, people in Starbuck built a 10-foot-by-10-foot (3-m-by-3-m) griddle. Eight bakers prepared dough made from 32 pounds (14.5 kg) of potatoes, 30 pounds (13.6 kg) of flour, 2 pounds (0.9 kg) of sugar, and 4 pounds (1.8 kg) of shortening. Then they baked the biggest lefse (potato pancake) on record. Each May, Starbuck celebrates this event.

7. MayDay Parade and Festival

This three-part event celebrates the arrival of spring. Held in Minneapolis in May, this event features a parade, ceremony, and festival. Thousands of people attend, and they enjoy food, music, and dancing.

8. Minnesota State Fair

Every year in late August and early September, St. Paul holds a state fair that brings the farms to the big city. Agricultural exhibits, animal shows, and baking contests share the stage with musical acts and industrial displays. There is also plenty of food on hand. The fair attracted 1.7 million people in 2013.

9. St. Paul Winter Carnival

In January, this city hosts the country's oldest and largest winter festival. Highlights include parades, contests, snow sculpting, a snow slide, and an ice palace.

10. *Wacipi*

"Wacipi," which means "dance" in Dakota, is an important part of the powwow held each year in Mankato in September. This event is one of several held there at which Native Americans celebrate their rich culture.

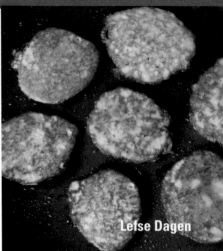

Lefse Dagen

Minnesota State Fair

St. Paul Winter Carnival

The State Capitol in St. Paul is a center of government and a Minnesota landmark.

How the Government Works

Many government workers serve Minnesota by helping to run the state's cities, townships, and counties. These are all different units of local government. Four out of five Minnesotans live in cities, although these cities take up only about 5 percent of the state's land area. Most of Minnesota's more than 800 cities are small, with between 1,000 and 10,000 people. About 100 are "charter cities." This means that they can decide, within limits, the type of local government that fits their needs and then write their own charter, or set of rules. The rest of the cities are called statutory cities. They follow the laws and guidelines that the state has adopted for local governments. Most Minnesota cities are governed by an elected city **council** and elected mayor. But in some cities, a city manager is hired by the elected council.

The state also has close to 1,800 townships. Many townships cover large rural areas that have small populations. Each township is governed by an elected board of supervisors that usually has three members. In townships, many important decisions are made by citizens themselves at an annual town meeting.

On a higher level, the state is divided into 87 counties. A five- or seven-member board of commissioners manages each county. Voters elect board members to four-year terms.

Members of the Minnesota House of Representatives meet here to debate and vote on the state's laws.

They also might elect a county attorney, recorder, sheriff, treasurer, and auditor for four-year terms. Along with the cities and townships, the counties provide a variety of important services to people in Minnesota.

Branches of Government

Executive

The executive branch is headed by the governor, who is elected to a four-year term. The lieutenant governor, secretary of state, auditor, and attorney general are also elected to four-year terms. The governor supervises the state government, plans the budget, and appoints other officials to help carry out the state's programs.

Legislative

The legislative branch makes the state's laws. It has two chambers, or parts: the Senate and the House of Representatives. The Senate has 67 members, elected for four-year terms (or for two-year terms in years ending in 0). The house has 134 members, elected for two-year terms.

Judicial

The judicial branch applies the state's laws in court cases and sometimes decides whether a law is allowed under the state constitution. At the lowest level, there about 300 district courts, hearing some 2 million cases a year. Their

These students visited the State Capitol and also had a chance to decide how they would vote on 12 different issues facing the state government.

U.S. Senator from Minnesota Al Franken talks with a student from Eden Prairie who was honored for his volunteer work.

rulings can be appealed to one of the nineteen appellate courts and then to the state Supreme Court. The Supreme Court, the state's highest court, has six associate justices and one chief justice. In Minnesota, all judges are elected. They serve six-year terms.

State and Federal Government

The state government, like the federal (national) government, is divided into three branches: executive, legislative, and judicial. The center of Minnesota's state government is the capital, St. Paul.

Minnesotans elect lawmakers to represent them in the U.S. Congress in Washington, D.C. Like all other states, Minnesota has two U.S. senators. The number of members a state sends to the U.S. House of Representatives is based on its population. As of 2014, Minnesota had eight representatives in the House.

How a Bill Becomes a Law

A bill is a proposed law or change in an existing law. Only someone from the legislative branch of government can start a bill on the process required for it to become state law.

The bill must first be presented, or introduced, by a senator or representative. From there, it goes to a committee of the Senate or house, wherever the bill's sponsor serves. After discussing the bill, committee members reject or approve it.

If the committee approves the bill, members of the whole chamber study and discuss it. Sometimes, they may change parts of the bill or add or remove parts of it. If the bill passes in the chamber where it was first proposed, it moves to the other chamber. Both chambers must pass the exact same bill before it can go to the governor. If the second chamber approves the bill but makes changes in it, the bill goes to a special committee in which members from both the House of Representatives and the Senate work to resolve the differences.

Once both chambers have passed the exact same bill by a majority vote, it goes to the governor. The governor can sign the bill, in which case it becomes law. The governor can also allow a bill to become law by taking no action on it. If the governor disagrees with the bill, he or she can veto, or reject, it. If the governor vetoes the bill, it goes back to the legislature, where it can be voted on again. It can still become law—but only if it is again passed by a two-thirds vote in both the house and the Senate.

Minnesota's state legislators have made new laws in many different areas, from energy and the environment to traffic, crime, education, and taxes. Many recent state laws are meant to help consumers and safeguard people's safety and health. For example, the legislature recently passed a law to ban the sale of unsafe toys. Another new measure protects consumers from having to pay for calls made when their cell phone is stolen. And another law set up a group to study how the state can help people with Alzheimer's disease.

POLITICAL FIGURES
FROM MINNESOTA

Sharon Sayles Belton
Mayor of Minneapolis, 1994-2001

Born in St. Paul, Belton has always been a community leader. She co-founded the Harriet Tubman Shelter for Battered Women in 1976. In 1983, she was elected to the Minneapolis City Council. Ten years later, she became the first African American and the first female mayor of Minneapolis, where she served two terms.

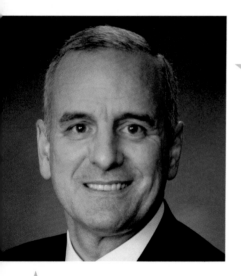

Mark Dayton
Governor of Minnesota, 2011-

Mark Dayton was born in Minneapolis, where he played hockey as a child. After graduating from Yale, Dayton taught science. He later served as an aide to Senator Walter Mondale, and became a U.S. Senator himself in 2000. Ten years later, Dayton was elected Governor of Minnesota.

Walter Mondale
U.S. Vice President, 1977-1981

Born in Ceylon, Mondale admired politicians at a young age. He graduated from the University of Minnesota, served in the U.S. Army, and earned a law degree. Mondale worked as a lawyer in Minneapolis, and was appointed U.S. Senator in 1964. Jimmy Carter chose him as his running mate, and Mondale became Vice President in 1977.

MINNESOTA
YOU CAN MAKE A DIFFERENCE

Contacting Lawmakers

To contact a member of the Minnesota state legislature, go to:

www.leg.state.mn.us

Look for the question "Who Represents Me?" near the bottom of the second column.

Put in your street address, city, and zip code, and click "search."

Select the person you want to contact and click on "MEMBER PAGE" for that person.

A Voice in Government

"Our government was founded on the idea that anyone can make a difference," writes a Minnesota government official. "If you think [that] issues won't be of interest until you're older, think again." Minnesotans must be 18 years old to vote. But that does not mean that younger people cannot have a say in what happens in their state and nation. Young Minnesotans find many ways to participate in government.

Project Citizen has civics programs for students in grades five to twelve. One program encourages students to work together to define a public problem. Then they think of ways to solve it and develop a plan to put their ideas to work. After writing the plan, students can send their report to be judged by legislators and community leaders. A number of middle-school students in Minnesota have participated in Project Citizen. One group recently worked on the issue of smoking in public. As part of the project, they followed the progress of the "Freedom to Breathe" bill as it made its way through the state legislature. This measure, which became a law and went into effect in 2007, banned smoking indoors in public places.

A farmer shows off some of his corn harvest.

Making a Living

Minnesota began as a farm state, and agriculture remains an important part of the economy, though farming itself does not account for many jobs. Minnesota's forests and mines are other important resources. Many businesses in Minnesota turn the state's crops and other natural resources and raw materials into goods that are then sold nationwide. One example is General Mills, based in Golden Valley, which makes more than 100 brands of food products, from Hamburger Helper to Cheerios.

Minnesota universities and businesses join together to create new products and improve old ones. Some common household items, including see-through adhesive tape and Post-it® notes, were invented in Minnesota. Retail stores employ many thousands of people in Minnesota. The largest shopping mall in the United States, the Mall of America, is located in Bloomington. But not all Minnesota jobs involve creating and selling goods. Many of the state's largest industries, including health care, education, and tourism, are service industries.

A farmer harvests soybeans near Worthington.

Farming in Minnesota

Minnesota is a major farm state. It is among the top four states for growing feed corn and soybeans—the state's most valuable crops. Minnesota is also a leading producer of wheat, oats, barley, potatoes, dried beans, and several seeds used in cooking oils and biodiesel fuels. Year after year, it is the number one grower of sugar beets, as well as of corn and peas for freezing or canning. Minnesota is also a key dairy state, and it is among the main states for raising and marketing pigs and for producing red meat. Finally, Minnesota raises more turkeys than any other state.

Minnesota vies with California as the nation's largest producer of cultivated wild rice. But California has no native beds of wild rice. In Minnesota, on the other hand, truly wild rice thrives in numerous lakes and marshes in large areas of the state. Native Americans continue to gather wild rice using traditional methods that are centuries old.

Farmers in Minnesota have had a long tradition of working together to grow and sell what they produce. To do this, they formed organizations called cooperatives, which help farmers reduce their costs and also can reduce prices for consumers. The idea of cooperatives can be traced back to Minnesota's Scandinavian immigrants. Today, there are hundreds of cooperatives in operation in the state, including grain elevators, energy suppliers, dairies, and many other kinds. Some of the state's most successful international businesses are still cooperatives.

People arrange vegetables at a farmers market in Minneapolis.

★10★KEY INDUSTRIES★

Banking

1. Banking

Minnesota is one of America's leading financial centers, offering banking, insurance, and investment services. In 2013, Minnesota had 360 commercial banks. That year, Minneapolis-St. Paul had one of the highest concentrations of banks in the U.S.

2. Biosciences

Minnesota is a leader in the **biosciences**, from medical devices to microbiology and industrial biotechnology. Minnesota is also home to the Mayo Clinic, the first and largest not-for-profit medical group practice in the world.

3. Computers and Electronics

Minnesota is a leader in producing and developing electronic equipment. Computers, medical instruments, telephones, and many other items are made in Minnesota factories and shipped around the world.

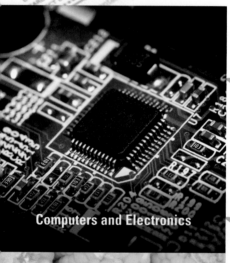
Computers and Electronics

4. Corn

Southern Minnesota sits in the Midwestern corn belt. This is where farms grow large amounts of corn. Most of Minnesota's corn is used to feed beef cattle, but some is canned or frozen and shipped to grocery stores around the world.

5. Dairy

With around 500,000 dairy cattle, Minnesota is a top milk supplier. With its productive dairy farms, the state is also a leading manufacturer of dairy goods, including butter and cheese.

Corn

MINNESOTA

6. Flour

Minnesota is a key state in turning wheat into flour. Minnesota companies make the flour into foods, such as breakfast cereals, cake mixes, and baked goods.

7. Iron

Large deposits of iron ore still lie in the Mesabi Range. Once the ore is mined, it is sent by truck or by train to a processing plant. There, the ore is ground into a fine powder, the iron is extracted by a magnet, and the iron powder is formed into marble-size pellets. The pellets are usually shipped from Duluth to steel mills along the Great Lakes or elsewhere around the world.

8. Pulp and Paper

Minnesota's forests provide timber for scrap board and paper products. Large paper mills can be found in such places as International Falls, Grand Rapids, Sartell, Cloquet, and Duluth.

9. Solar Energy

Minnesota has experienced growth in solar energy projects, both large and small, that employ a large number of residents. A goal for the state is for 25 percent of its electricity to come from renewable energy sources by 2025.

10. Wind Power

Minnesota ranked seventh in the nation in wind capacity in 2012. The state has more than 100 companies that produce wind power components, including turbines, motors, and other parts.

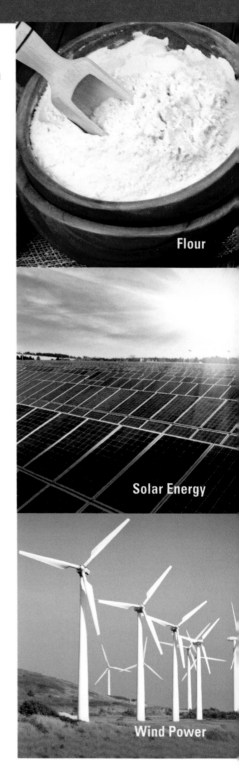

Flour

Solar Energy

Wind Power

Recipe for Blueberry Muffins

Blueberries are native to Northeast Minnesota. They grow in forested areas, bogs, and hillsides. It's no wonder blueberry muffins became the state muffin! Now, with a little help from an adult, you can make blueberry muffins of your own. Enjoy them for breakfast or as a snack!

What You Need

1 cup (120 grams) flour

1 cup (90 g) oatmeal

3 tbsp (37 g) sugar

1 tsp (5 milliliters) salt

4 tsp (20 ml) baking powder

1 cup (150 g) blueberries, washed

1 egg

1 cup (240 ml) milk

¼ cup (60 ml) vegetable oil

nonstick cooking spray

What To Do

- Preheat oven to 400°F (200°C).
- In a large bowl, mix together the flour, oatmeal, sugar, salt, and baking powder.
- Mix in blueberries.
- In another bowl, break the egg, and use a fork to lightly beat it.
- Add milk and vegetable oil, and mix.
- Add egg mixture to the dry ingredients in the large bowl.
- Using a mixing spoon, mix about 25 or 30 times. Leave the mixture lumpy.
- Line a muffin tin with paper liners or lightly spray with nonstick spray.
- Using a spoon, fill each muffin cup about 2/3 of the way up with the mix.
- Bake for about 20 minutes.
- When muffins are finished baking, remove from muffin tin and cool them on a wire rack.
- Enjoy!

Minnesota Manufacturing

Making crops into food products is a leading business in Minnesota, and the state is home to some of the world's biggest food-processing companies. For example, General Mills started in the 1860s as a flour mill on the Mississippi River. Land O' Lakes started in the 1920s as a cooperative to sell butter. Hormel Foods began as a meatpacking company in the 1890s and in the 1930s became famous for its canned meats. Today, these companies sell their original products, as well as hundreds of other packaged foods, throughout the world.

Minnesota's forests are important in the state's industries. Loggers manage the forests, harvesting trees for manufacturing paper and paper products, as well as for furniture and construction materials. In recent years, Minnesota has ranked first among all the states in the manufacture of wooden doors and windows.

Minnesota is also a leader in manufacturing many kinds of high-tech equipment. Factories turn out everything from supercomputers and computer software to the latest medical devices and supplies. Important healthcare breakthroughs include blood pumps, pacemakers for damaged hearts, and hearing aids.

Mining in Minnesota

Mining has been an important industry in Minnesota for more than a hundred years. At one time, high-grade iron ore accounted for most of the mining industry. By the 1950s, however, most of this ore had been mined. Mining companies then turned their attention to a low-grade ore called taconite. They developed new methods to extract iron from taconite. To this day, Minnesota remains the nation's main supplier of iron ore. In recent years, Minnesota has also been the nation's leading producer of cut stone. Quarries in different parts of the state mine granite, limestone, sandstone, and other kinds of stone used as building materials.

Services, Sales, and Tourism

The largest number of Minnesotans work in service industries, such as hospitals, schools, insurance agencies, utility companies, transportation and shipping firms, banks and other financial institutions, government agencies, hotels, restaurants, and stores of all kinds.

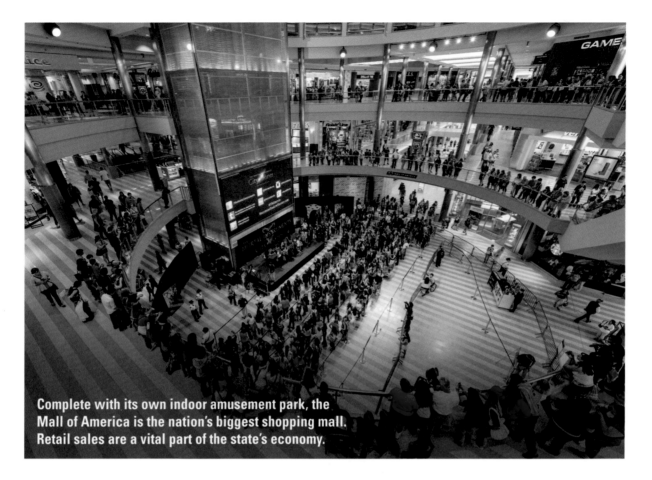

Complete with its own indoor amusement park, the Mall of America is the nation's biggest shopping mall. Retail sales are a vital part of the state's economy.

Wholesale and retail sales are important to Minnesota's economy. For example, some 11,000 people work at the Mall of America. With more than 500 stores and an indoor amusement park, the mall is the largest in the country. Besides selling products, the mall is part of Minnesota's tourist industry. It attracts around 40 million visitors every year—more than the Grand Canyon, Walt Disney World, and Elvis Presley's home, Graceland, combined.

Another important tourist attraction is the outdoors. Minnesotans and visitors alike enjoy the state's waters, woods, and fields. More than a million fishing licenses are sold every year, and there is one boat for every six people in the state. In fact, water skis were invented by a Minnesotan. Fans of winter sports love to skate, ski, snowboard, or ride across the winter landscape on snowmobiles. The first snowmobile was invented in Minnesota as well. The state's government has made efforts to regulate tourism so as to preserve the environment while still allowing Minnesotans the opportunity to fully enjoy the state's natural beauty and many opportunities for recreation. One example of regulation is the rule that allows only nonmotorized boats in the Boundary Waters Canoe Area Wilderness.

Besides participating in outdoor sports, visitors and residents like to root for the state's professional sports teams. Minnesota's Major League Baseball team is the Twins, named after the Twin Cities. Fans cheer on the Minnesota Vikings during the National Football League season. The Lynx are the Women's National Basketball Association team, while the men's National Basketball Association team is the Timberwolves.

In the year 2000, seven years after the Minnesota North Stars moved away, the state again got a National Hockey League team of its own, the Wild. There are also hundreds of recreational and school hockey teams in Minnesota. With their love of winter sports and their huge supply of winter ice and snow, it is no wonder that Minnesotans have named ice hockey the official state sport.

The Minnesota Gophers are the University of Minnesota's hockey team.

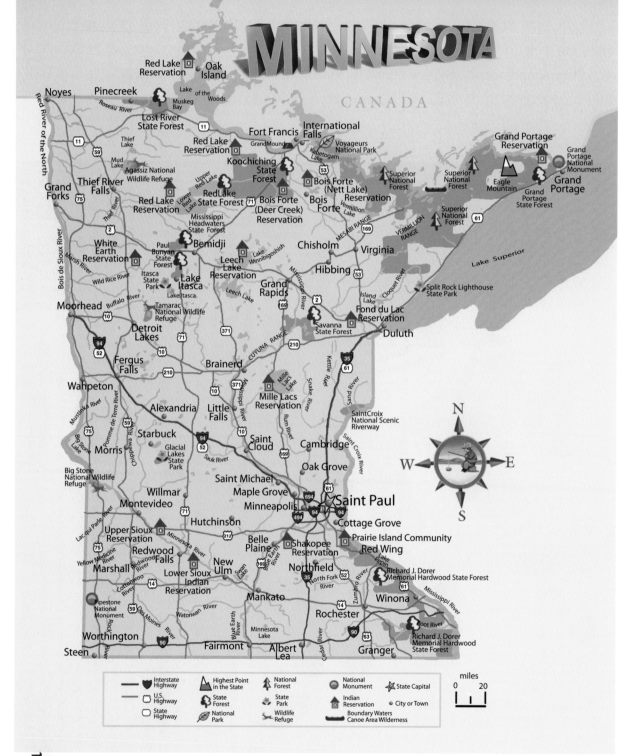

MINNESOTA

CANADA

Noyes
Pinecreek
Red Lake Reservation
Oak Island
Lake of the Woods
Muskeg Bay
Roseau River
Lost River State Forest
Fort Francis
International Falls
GrandMound
Voyageurs National Park
Kabetogam Lake
Thief Lake
Mud Lake
Agassiz National Wildlife Refuge
Red Lake Reservation
Koochiching State Forest
Bois Forte (Nett Lake) Reservation
Superior National Forest
Superior National Forest
Grand Portage Reservation
Grand Portage National Monument
Eagle Mountain
Grand Portage State Forest
Grand Portage
Thief River Falls
Upper Red Lake
RedLake State Forest
Bois Forte (Deer Creek) Reservation
Bois Forte
Vermillion Lake
Superior National Forest
Grand Forks
Lower Red Lake
Red Lake Reservation
Mississippi Headwaters State Forest
MESABI RANGE
VERMILLION RANGE
White Earth Reservation
Paul Bunyan State Forest
Bemidji
Lake Winnibigoshish
Chisholm
Virginia
Lake Superior
Wild Rice River
Itasca State Park
Leech Lake Reservation
Hibbing
Island Lake
Cloquet River
Split Rock Lighthouse State Park
Moorhead
Lake Itasca
Leech Lake
Grand Rapids
Mississippi River
Fond du Lac Reservation
Buffalo River
Tamarac National Wildlife Refuge
Savanna State Forest
Duluth
Detroit Lakes
Brainerd
Kettle River
Fergus Falls
Mille Lacs Lake
Snake River
Saint Croix River
Wahpeton
Alexandria
Little Falls
Mille Lacs Reservation
SaintCroix National Scenic Riverway
Starbuck
Glacial Lakes State Park
Sauk River
Saint Cloud
Rum River
Cambridge
Morris
Big Stone Lake
Big Stone National Wildlife Refuge
Willmar
Montevideo
Saint Michael
Maple Grove
Minneapolis
Oak Grove
Saint Paul
Cottage Grove
Hutchinson
Upper Sioux Reservation
Minnesota River
Belle Plaine
Shakopee Reservation
Prairie Island Community
Red Wing
Redwood Falls
New Ulm
Northfield
Lake Pepin
Marshall
Lower Sioux Indian Reservation
Swan Lake
North Fork River
Richard J. Dorer Memorial Hardwood State Forest
Mankato
Winona
Mississippi River
Pipestone National Monument
Rochester
Worthington
Minnesota Lake
Richard J. Dorer Memorial Hardwood State Forest
Root River
Steen
Fairmont
Albert Lea
Granger

Legend

Interstate Highway	Highest Point in the State	National Forest	National Monument	State Capital			
U.S. Highway	State Forest	State Park	Indian Reservation	City or Town			
State Highway	National Park	Wildlife Refuge	Boundary Waters Canoe Area Wilderness				

miles
0   20

MINNESOTA
MAP SKILLS

1. What is Minnesota's highest point?

2. Which interstate takes you from Moorhead to Saint Paul?

3. What is Minnesota's northernmost reservation?

4. Which river runs along the state's western border?

5. What national monument can be found in the southwestern corner of the state?

6. Which two lakes are located west of Grand Rapids?

7. Which State highway runs between Wahpeton and Duluth?

8. Which national park borders Canada?

9. Mud Lake and Agassiz National Wildlife Refuge are located northeast of what city?

10. Which U.S. highway runs north-south through the center of the state?

Duluth

Minnehaha Falls

St. Paul

10. U.S. Highway 71
9. Thief River Falls
8. Voyageurs National Park
7. State Highway 210
6. Lake Winnibigoshish and Leech Lake
5. Pipestone National Monument
4. Bois de Sioux River
3. Red Lake Reservation
2. Interstate 94
1. Eagle Mountain

State Seal, Flag, and Song

The state seal shows a farmer in a field of grain near the Mississippi River and a Native American on horseback. The state motto, "Star of the North," appears in French over the scene. The sun symbolizes Minnesota's flat plains. The Native American's horse, the axe, rifle, and plow represent tools that were used throughout the state's history. The stump symbolizes the importance of the lumber industry in Minnesota. The Mississippi River and St. Anthony Falls represent the importance of these resources in transportation and industry. The cultivated ground and the plow symbolize the importance of agriculture to the state.

Minnesota's flag is royal blue with a seal (almost identical to the state seal) in the center. A wreath appears around the seal. The wreath displays the state flower along with three years: 1819 (the year Fort Snelling was established), 1858 (the year of statehood), and 1893 (the year the first flag was adopted). Because Minnesota was the nineteenth state admitted after the original thirteen states, nineteen stars are on the flag.

To see the lyrics of the Minnesota State Song, "Hail! Minnesota," go to **www.statesymbolsusa.org/Minnesota/stateSONG**

Glossary

archaeologists   People who study past human life and activities by studying the bones, tools, etc., of ancient people.

biosciences   Sciences that deal with the biological aspects of living organisms.

conservatory   A room or building with glass walls and a glass roof that is used for growing plants.

council   A group of people who are chosen to make rules, laws, or decisions about something.

custom   An action or way of behaving that is usual and traditional among the people in a particular group or place.

ecosystem   Everything that exists in a particular environment.

endangered   At risk of no longer existing.

execution   The act of killing someone especially as punishment for a crime.

fertile   Able to support the growth of many plants.

immigrants   People who come to a country to live there.

imported   Brought into a country to be sold.

legislature   A group of people with the power to make or change laws.

migration   The movement from one place to another.

minorities   People who are different from a larger group of people.

missionary   A person who is sent to a foreign country to do religious work.

plague   A destructively numerous amount.

More About Minnesota

BOOKS

Dwyer, Helen, and Sierra Adare. *Ojibwe History and Culture*. New York, NY: Gareth Stevens Publishing, 2012.

Goessling, Ben. *Minnesota Timberwolves*. Minneapolis, MN: SportsZone, 2011.

Heinrichs, Ann. *Minnesota*. New York, NY: Scholastic, 2014.

MacRae, Sloan. *The Minnesota Twins*. New York, NY: PowerKids Press, 2011.

Purslow, Neil. *Minnesota: The North Star State*. New York, NY: Av2 by Weigl, 2011.

WEBSITES

Minnesota Department of Natural Resources:

www.dnr.state.mn.us

Minnesota Department of Tourism:

www.exploreminnesota.com

State of Minnesota Official Website:

www.state.mn.gov

ABOUT THE AUTHORS

Marlene Targ Brill writes about many topics, from history and biographies to sports, world peace, and health issues. Each of her more than 50 books takes her on another journey, where she sees exciting places and meets interesting people. Minnesota is one of those places. Before launching her writing career, she taught students with special needs and teachers learning to work with them. She and her family live in Illinois.

Elizabeth Kaplan has edited textbooks and reference works on a wide variety of subjects. She has also written several science and social studies books for young adults. Throughout her life, she has enjoyed going on road trips. In her travels, she has been to 47 of the 50 states, including Minnesota. She lives in Wisconsin with her husband and two daughters.

Index

Page numbers in **boldface** are illustrations.

Index